PLUTO
and the Dwarf Planets

by Ellen Lawrence

Consultants:

Suzy Gazlay, MA
Recipient, Presidential Award for Excellence in Science Teaching

Kevin Yates
Fellow of the Royal Astronomical Society

Published in 2014 by Ruby Tuesday Books Ltd.

Editor: Mark J. Sachner
Designer: Emma Randall

Photo Credits:
European Southern Observatory: 11 (bottom); NASA:
4 (bottom), 6, 11 (top), 12–13, 14–15, 16–17, 18–19, 20
(center); Ruby Tuesday Books: 7, 9, 22; Science Photo
Library: 4–5; Superstock: Cover, 10, 20 (bottom), 21.

Library of Congress Control Number: 2013939989

ISBN 978-1-909673-20-5

Printed and published in the United States of America

For further information including rights and
permissions requests, please contact our Customer
Service Department at 877-337-8577.

Contents

Words shown in **bold** in the text are
explained in the glossary.

Welcome to Pluto

Imagine flying to a world that is billions of miles from Earth.

In every direction, the land is covered with ice.

On this tiny, faraway world, it is much colder than the coldest place on Earth.

Welcome to the **dwarf planet**, Pluto!

Pluto

Earth

Mars

A dwarf planet is a small, round space object. Dwarf planets are much smaller than big **planets**, such as Earth and Mars.

Charon

The Sun

The surface
of Pluto

This picture shows what it might look like on the surface of Pluto. Earth, our home planet, has one **moon**, but tiny Pluto has five! Pluto's largest moon is called Charon (KARE-uhn).

The Solar System

Pluto is moving in a huge circle around the Sun.

Other dwarf planets are **orbiting**, or moving, around the Sun, too.

There are also eight big planets circling the Sun.

The big planets are called Mercury, Venus, our home planet Earth, Mars, Jupiter, Saturn, Uranus, and Neptune.

Together, the planets, dwarf planets, and other space objects are called the **solar system**.

Icy **comets** and space rocks called **asteroids** also circle the Sun. Most of the asteroids are in a ring called the **asteroid belt**.

An asteroid

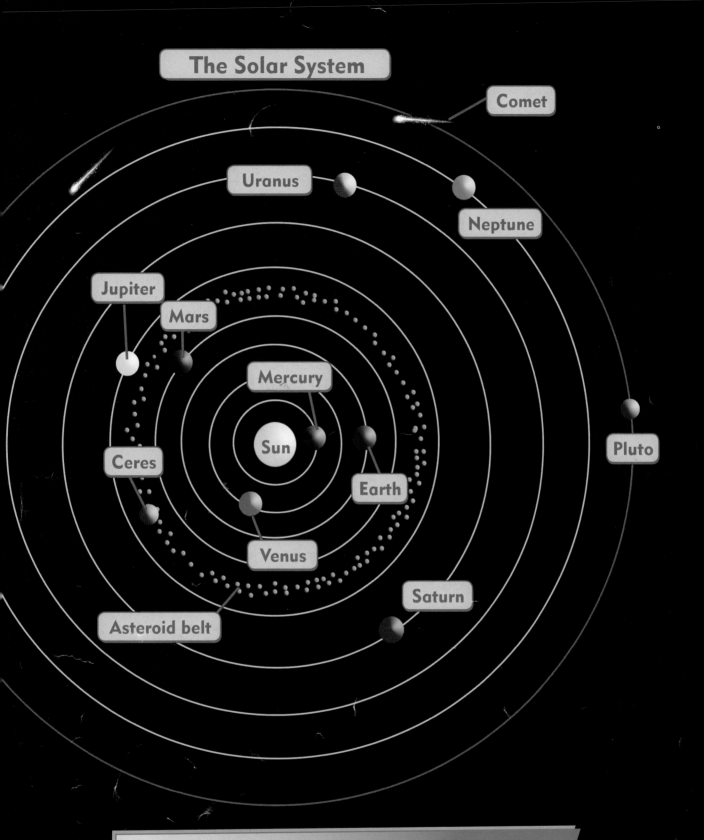

The Solar System

Comet

Uranus

Neptune

Jupiter

Mars

Mercury

Sun

Ceres

Earth

Venus

Pluto

Saturn

Asteroid belt

Two dwarf planets, Pluto and Ceres, can be seen in this diagram. Other dwarf planets are moving through space beyond Pluto.

Meet the Dwarf Planets

For many years, Pluto was called a planet.

Then, scientists began to discover other small objects like Pluto orbiting far away from the Sun.

They decided to put these small objects into their own group and call them dwarf planets.

At the end of 2012, the dwarf planet group had five members.

They are named Pluto, Eris, Ceres, Makemake, and Haumea.

Scientists think there are still more dwarf planets to be discovered.

Dwarf Planet Names

Here's how to say the dwarf planets' names:
Ceres (SIHR-eez)
Eris (IHR-iss)
Haumea (how-MEH-uh)
Makemake (MAH-kee-MAH-kee)
Pluto (PLOO-toh)

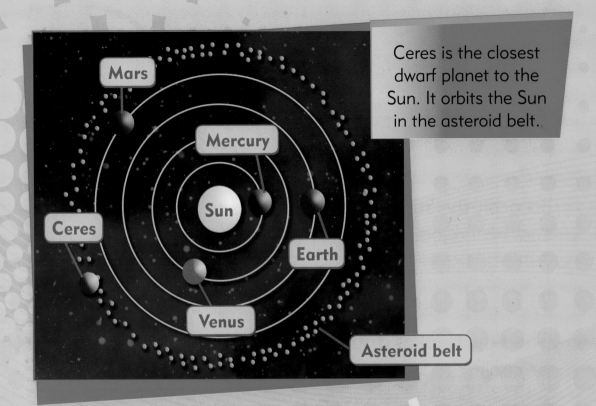

Mars

Mercury

Sun

Ceres

Earth

Venus

Asteroid belt

Ceres is the closest dwarf planet to the Sun. It orbits the Sun in the asteroid belt.

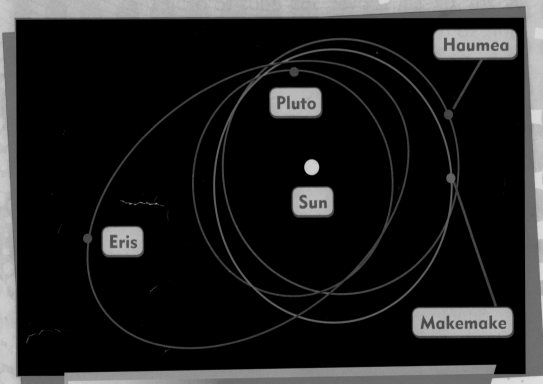

Haumea

Pluto

Sun

Eris

Makemake

Pluto, Eris, Makemake, and Haumea are billions of miles from the Sun. This picture shows the shapes of their journeys around the Sun.

A Closer Look at Pluto

To orbit the Sun once, Pluto makes a super-long journey.

It travels through space for nearly 23 billion miles (37 billion km).

The time it takes a space object to orbit, or circle, the Sun once is called its year.

Earth takes just over 365 days to orbit the Sun, so a year on Earth lasts 365 days.

It takes Pluto almost 248 Earth years to orbit the Sun.

This means a year on Pluto lasts for 248 Earth years!

Pluto

As a dwarf planet orbits the Sun, it also **rotates**, or spins, like a top.

Pluto is 1,430 miles wide (2,302 km). Its largest moon, Charon, is about half this size.

Pluto

Charon

The Sun

Pluto

This picture shows how it might look to stand on Pluto. The faraway Sun looks like a tiny, shining dot!

Faraway Eris

As it orbits the Sun, Eris is sometimes 97 times farther from the Sun than Earth.

It takes this dwarf planet 560 Earth years to orbit the Sun once!

It is difficult for scientists to study Eris because it is so far from Earth.

They know it is super-cold because it is so far from the Sun's heat.

They also think it is about the same size as Pluto, but no one knows for sure.

This picture shows how Eris might look. It has one moon, called Dysnomia (dis-NOH-mee-uh). There may be more moons to be discovered, though.

The Sun

Dysnomia

Eris

Makemake and Haumea

Haumea is a rocky, icy, egg-shaped dwarf planet.

It takes 283 Earth years to orbit the Sun once.

Makemake's journey around the Sun lasts for 307 Earth years!

Pluto, Eris, Haumea, and Makemake orbit the Sun in an area called the Kuiper Belt (KY-pur BELT).

The Kuiper Belt is a giant ring where thousands of icy space objects are gathered.

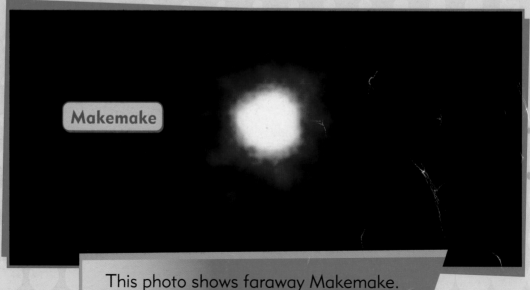

This photo shows faraway Makemake.
This dwarf planet is covered with ice.

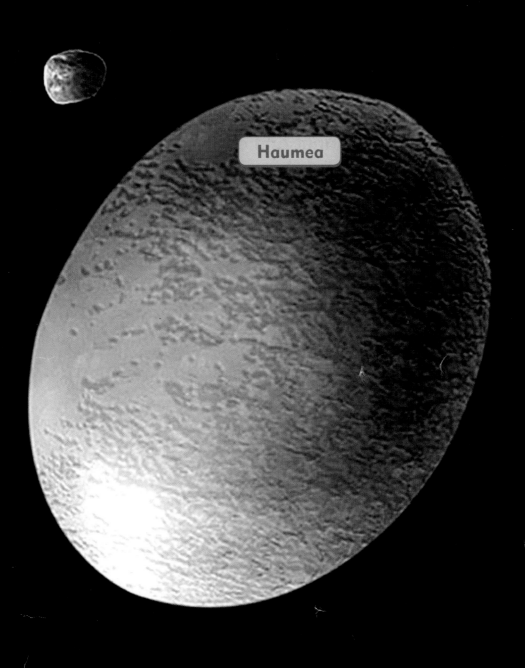

Haumea

Moon

Scientists have found two moons around Haumea, but there may be more. This picture shows what Haumea and its moons might look like.

Meet Ceres

Ceres is both a dwarf planet and an asteroid.

This large, rocky object is circling the Sun in the asteroid belt.

Ceres is much nearer to the Sun than the other dwarf planets.

It takes just over four and a half Earth years to orbit the Sun once.

Ceres is about 600 miles (966 km) wide.

That's almost as wide as Texas!

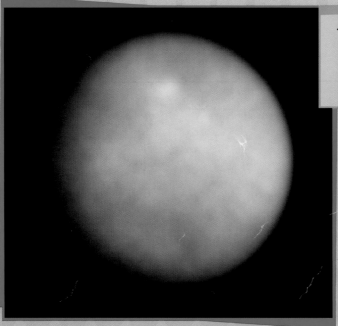

This is a photo of Ceres. It is the biggest asteroid in the asteroid belt.

Ceres

Earth

This picture shows the size of Ceres compared to Earth.

A Mission to Pluto

In January 2006, a space **probe** named *New Horizons* blasted off from Earth.

It will fly through space for over nine years and reach Pluto in 2015.

New Horizons will make a **flyby** of Pluto.

As it flies past the dwarf planet and its moons, it will take photos and collect information.

The probe will then make flybys of other objects in the Kuiper Belt.

New Horizons may even discover some new dwarf planets!

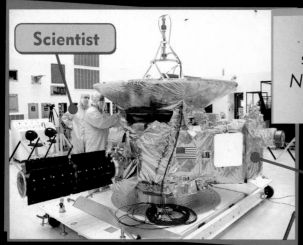

Scientist

This photo shows scientists working on *New Horizons* before its mission began.

New Horizons

This picture shows how *New Horizons* might look as it makes its flyby of Pluto.

Charon

Pluto

New Horizons

19

Pluto Fact File

Here are some key facts about Pluto, the most famous dwarf planet.

Discovery of Pluto

Pluto was discovered on February 18, 1930, by Clyde W. Tombaugh.

How Pluto got its name

Pluto is named after the Roman god of the underworld and afterlife.

Planet sizes

Here are the sizes of the solar system's eight big planets compared to Pluto.

Sun · Mercury · Earth · Venus · Mars · Jupiter · Saturn · Uranus · Neptune · Pluto

Pluto's size

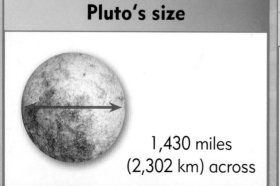

1,430 miles (2,302 km) across

How long it takes for Pluto to rotate once

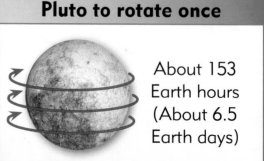

About 153 Earth hours (About 6.5 Earth days)

Pluto's distance from the Sun

The closest Pluto gets to the Sun is 2,756,872,958 miles (4,436,756,954 km).

The farthest Pluto gets from the Sun is 4,583,311,152 miles (7,376,124,302 km).

Length of Pluto's orbit around the Sun

22,698,676,007 miles (36,529,978,039 km)

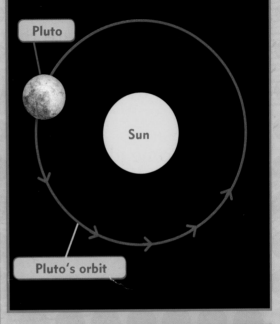

Pluto

Sun

Pluto's orbit

Average speed at which Pluto orbits the Sun

10,444 miles per hour (16,809 km/h)

Length of a year on Pluto

Over 90,553 Earth days (Nearly 248 Earth years)

Pluto's Moons

Pluto has at least five moons. There are possibly more to be discovered.

Temperature on Pluto

-378°F (-228°C)

Get Crafty
Make an Icy
Pluto Collage

Create a collage picture that shows Pluto in the icy Kuiper Belt. You can add in the faraway Sun, too.

Here are some ideas for things you could use to make a collage:

- Scraps of colored paper or cardboard
- Tissue paper or gift-wrap paper
- Glitter

Here are some items you might need when making your collage:

- A large sheet of thin cardboard or construction paper for the background
- Scissors
- White glue
- A paintbrush for spreading glue

Here's one example of a Pluto collage, but you can create your own. Think about:

- How will you show Pluto's icy surface?
- What will you use to make the icy objects in the Kuiper Belt?

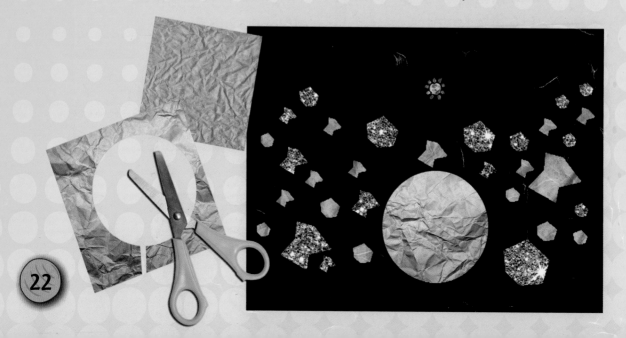

asteroid (AS-teh-royd) A large rock that is orbiting the Sun. An asteroid can be as small as a car or bigger than a mountain.

asteroid belt (AS-teh-royd BELT) A huge ring of asteroids that are orbiting the Sun.

comet (KAH-mit) A space object made of ice, rock, and dust that is orbiting the Sun.

dwarf planet (DWARF PLAN-et) A round object in space that is orbiting the Sun. Dwarf planets are much smaller than the eight main planets.

flyby (FLY-by) A flight by a spacecraft past a planet, moon, or other body in space. A flyby takes the spacecraft near the planet in order to study it closely and send information back to Earth.

moon (MOON) An object in space that is orbiting a planet. Moons are usually made of rock, or rock and ice. Some are just a few miles wide. Others are hundreds of miles wide.

orbit (OR-bit) To circle, or move around, another object.

planet (PLAN-et) A large object in space that is orbiting the Sun. Some planets, such as Earth and Mars, are made of rock. Others, such as Jupiter, are made of gases and liquids.

probe (PROBE) A spacecraft that does not have any people aboard. Probes are usually sent to planets or other objects in space to take photographs and collect information. They are controlled by scientists on Earth.

rotate (ROH-tate) To spin around.

solar system (SOH-ler SIS-tem) The Sun and all the objects that orbit it, such as planets, their moons, asteroids, and comets.

Index

Read More

Hughes, Catherine D. *First Big Book of Space (National Geographic Little Kids).* Washington, D.C.: The National Geographic Society (2012).

Winrich, Ralph, and Thomas K. Adamson (rev.) *Pluto: A Dwarf Planet (First Facts: The Solar System).* Mankato, MN: Capstone Press (2008).

Learn More Online

To learn more about Pluto and other dwarf planets, go to
www.rubytuesdaybooks.com/dwarfplanets